DATE:

TIME:

LOCATION:

Tape Your
Photo Here

PICTURE OF ME

Attach
Party
Invitation
Here

A is for

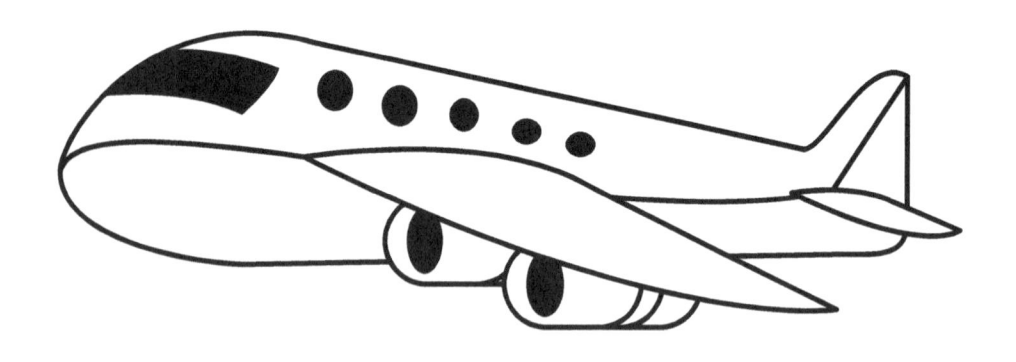

Airplane

With love, _____

B

is for

Backpack

With love, _____

C is for

Chair

With love, _____

D is for

Deer

With love, _____

E   is for

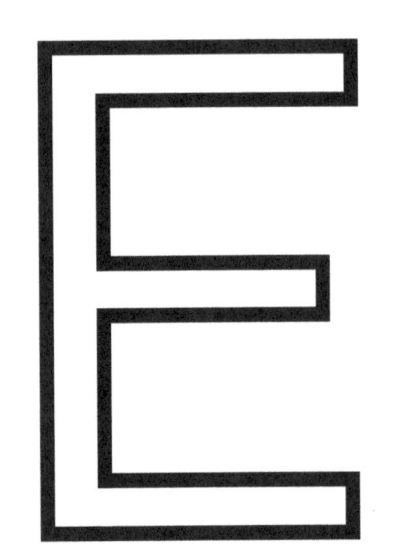

Evergreen

With love, _____

F is for

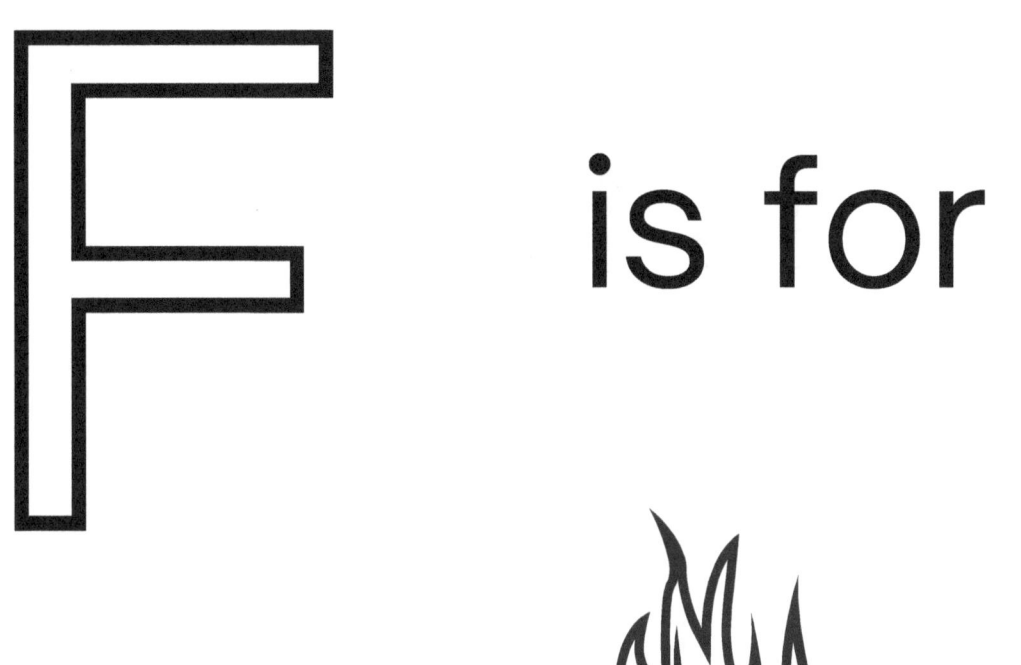

Fire

With love, _____

G is for

Grass

With love, _____

H   is for

Hat

With love, _____

I is for

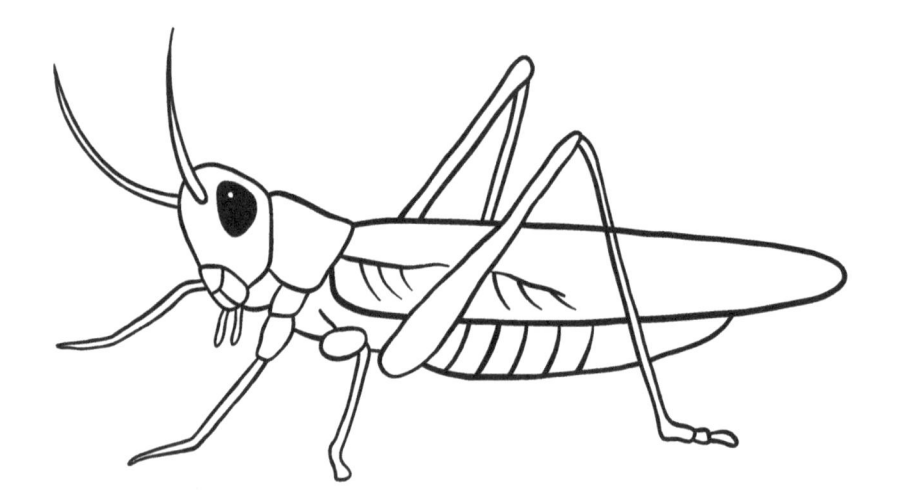

Insect

With love, _____

J   is for

Jupitar

With love, _____

K is for

Kettle

With love,_____

L

is for

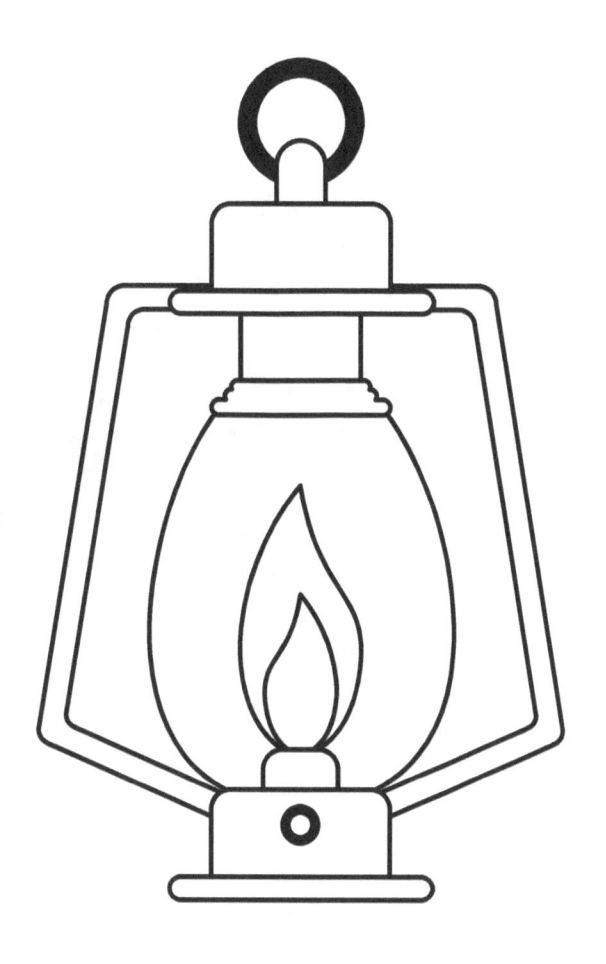

Lantern

With love, _____

M is for

Mountain

With love, _____

N is for

Nest

With love, _____

O is for

Owl

With love, _____

P   is for

Path

With love, _____

Q is for

Quilt

With love, _____

R is for

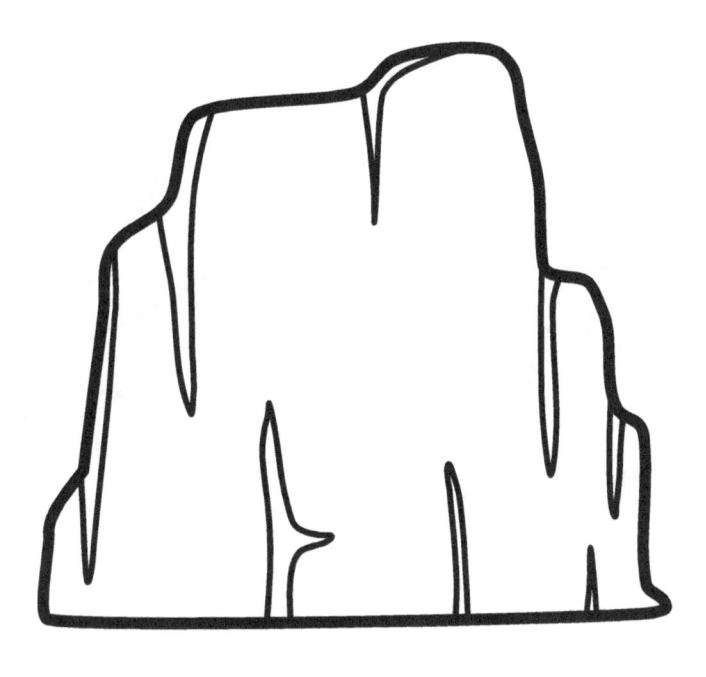

Rock

With love, _____

T is for

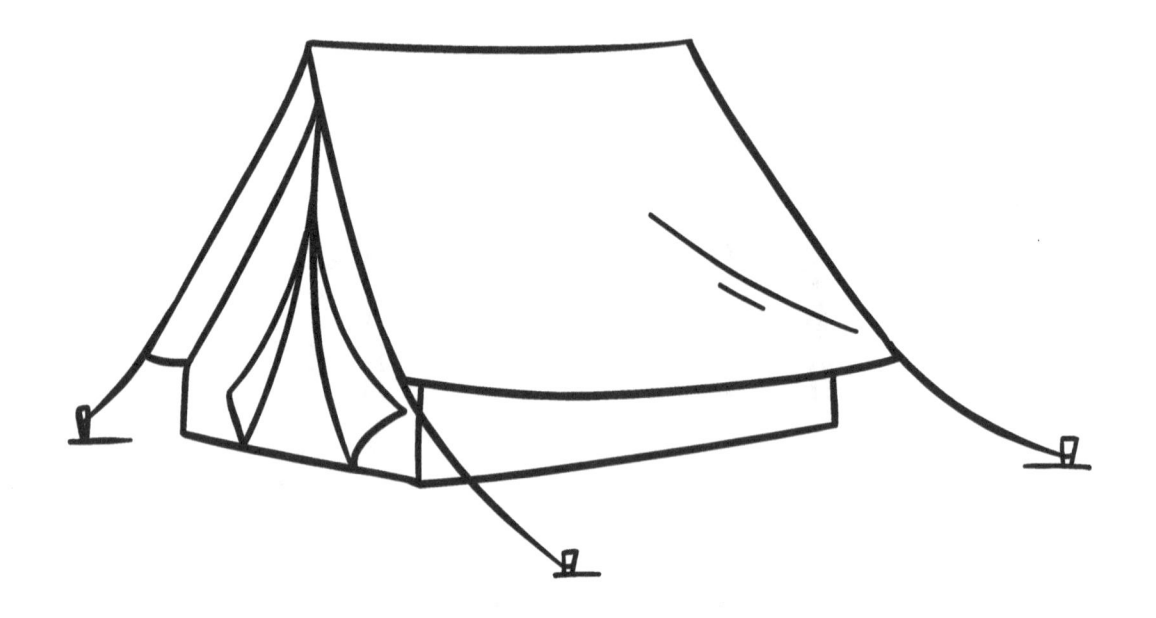

Tent

With love, _____

S is for

Shoe

With love, _____

U   is for

Umbrella

With love, _____

V is for

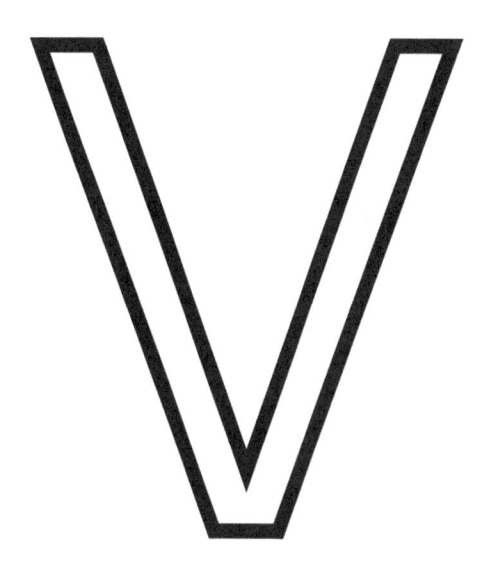

View

With love, _____

W is for

Wood

With love, _____

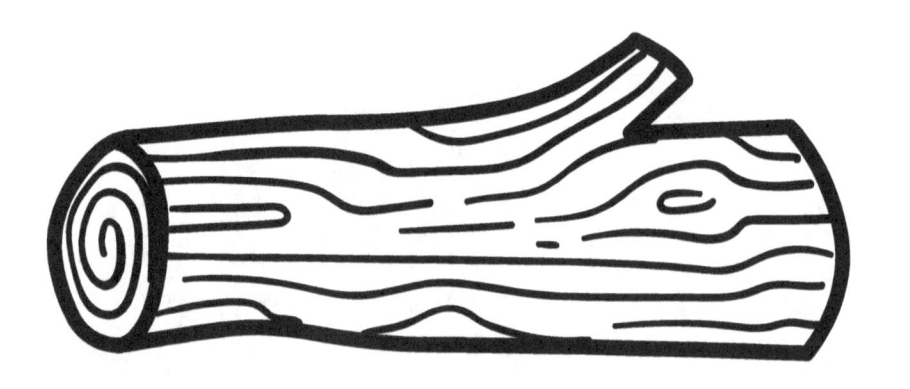

X

is for

X-ray

With love, _____

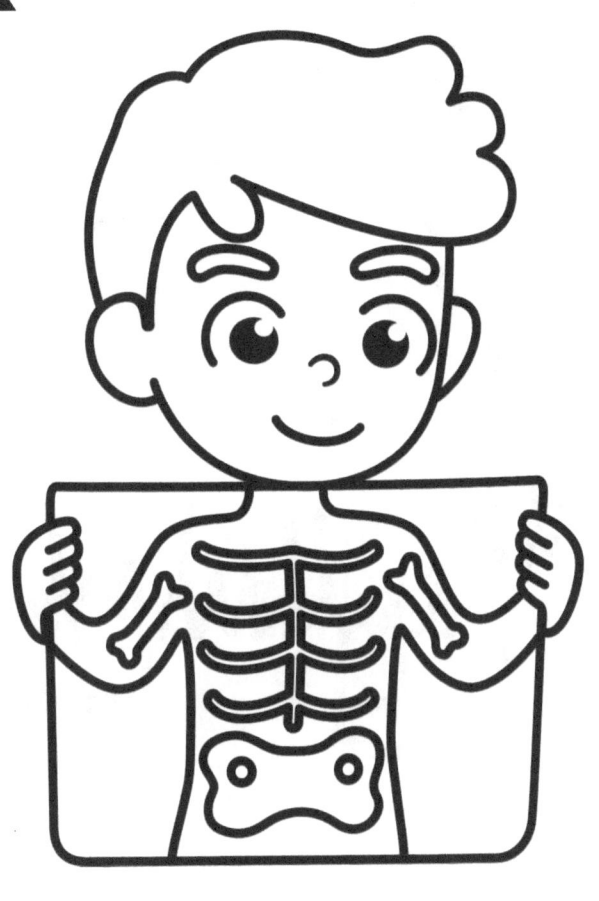

Y is for

Yak

With love, _____

Z is for

Zebra

With love, _____

GIFTS RECEIVED

Name _____
Gift Given _____

Name _____
Gift Given _____

Name _____
Gift Given _____

Name _____
Gift Given _____

Name _____
Gift Given _____

Name _____
Gift Given _____

Name _____
Gift Given _____

Name _____
Gift Given _____

Name _____
Gift Given _____

Name _____
Gift Given _____

Name _____
Gift Given _____

Name _____
Gift Given _____

Name _____
Gift Given _____

Name _____
Gift Given _____

Name _____
Gift Given _____

Name _____
Gift Given _____

Name _____
Gift Given _____

Name _____
Gift Given _____

Name _____
Gift Given _____

Name _____
Gift Given _____

Name _____
Gift Given _____

Name _____
Gift Given _____

Name _____
Gift Given _____

Name _____
Gift Given _____

Name _____
Gift Given _____

Name _____
Gift Given _____

Name _____
Gift Given _____

Name _____
Gift Given _____

Name _____
Gift Given _____

Name _____
Gift Given _____

Name _____
Gift Given _____

Name _____
Gift Given _____

Name _____
Gift Given _____

Name _____
Gift Given _____

Name _____
Gift Given _____

Name _____
Gift Given _____

Name _____
Gift Given _____

Name _____
Gift Given _____

Name _____
Gift Given _____

Name _____
Gift Given _____

Name _____
Gift Given _____

Name _____
Gift Given _____

PICTURES

My Favorite People

My Favorite People

My Favorite People

My Favorite People

My Favorite People

My Favorite People

My Favorite People

My Favorite People

MEMORIES

MEMORIES

MEMORIES

Baby Predictions

What is the date you think the baby will be born? _____ Month

_____ Day

What will be the babies weight at birth? _____ lbs _____ oz

How long will the baby be at birth? _____ Inches

What color eyes will the baby have? _____

What color hair will the baby have? _____

What will the baby's favorite food be? _____

What will the baby's first word be? _____

When will the baby first start walking? _____ Month _____ Day

What personality trait do you think the baby will have? _____

We would love to have your feedback.
Congratulations!

★ ★ ★ ★ ★

Scan Me

2022©Keeping Kids Creative All Rights Reserved
This book is copyright protected and only for personal use.
No part of this book may be reproduced or transmitted in any
form or by any means, electronic or mechanical, including
photocopying, recording, or by any other form without written
permission from the author and publisher.

Made in United States
Troutdale, OR
04/08/2025

30460528R00031